HEALTHY BODY

D0353224

Puberty and Your Body

Alison Cooper

WAYLAND

This book is based on the original title *How Does Adolescence Affect Me?* by Jenny Bryan, in the *Health and Fitness* series, published in 1999 by Hodder Wayland

This differentiated text edition is written by Alison Cooper and published in Great Britain in 2005 by Hodder Wayland, an imprint of Hodder Children's Books.

This paperback edition published by Wayland in 2007, an imprint of Hachette Children's Books.

Editor: Kirsty Hamilton
Designer: Jane Hawkins
Consultant: Jayne Wright

Picture acknowledgments:
Image Bank 10 (David de Lossy), 15 (Joe Patronite), 18 (Nicholas Russell), 31 (John Banagan), 38 (David de Lossy); Stock Market 6 (Charles Gupton), 16 (Mug Shots), 20 (Michael Keller), 26 (Michael Keller), 28 (Tom & DeeAnn McCarthy), 30, 39 (Jose L Pelaez Inc), 41, 42; Science Photo Library 9 (Profs PM Motta & Jvan Blerkom), 12 (Dr Yorgas Nikas), 14 (Cordelia Molloy), 17 (D Philips), 19 (Oscar Burriel/Lation Stock), 23 (Will & Deni McIntyre); Tony Stone Images 1 (Lori Adamski Peek), 4 (Peter Cade), 5 (Lee Page), 7 (Lori Adamski Peek), 13 (Roseanne Olson), 22 (Mary Kate Denny), 25 (Bruce Ayres), 27 (Ben Edwards), 29 (Eric Larravadieu), 32 (Terry Vine), 33 (Donna Day), 34 (Dan Sherwood), 35 (David Young Wolff), 36 (Nancy Honey), 37 (Peter Correz), 40 (Timothy Shonnard), 43 (Nick Vedros/Vedros & Associates), 44 (David Young Wolff), 45 (Lori Adamski Peek); The artwork on pages 8, 11 and 24 is by Michael Posen.

All possible care has been taken to trace the ownership of each photograph and to obtain permission for its use. If there are any omissions or if any errors have occurred, they will be corrected in subsequent editions, on notification to the publisher.

British Library Cataloguing in Publication Data
Cooper, Alison, 1967 -
Puberty and your body. - Differentiated ed. - (Healthy body)
1. Puberty - Juvenile literature
I. Title
612. 6'61

ISBN-13: 978 0 7502 5088 7

Printed in China

Wayland,
an imprint of Hachette Children's Books
338 Euston Road, London NW1 3BH

Contents

What is Puberty?

At around the age of ten you begin to develop from a child to an adult. Changes that take place inside your body mean that you become capable of producing a baby. These changes are called puberty.

Puberty marks the beginning of a longer stage of growth and development called adolescence. Doctors say that adolescence ends when a young person reaches their adult height and stops growing.

◀ There are some new challenges to tackle in adolescence – but if you are prepared for them they won't become problems.

For many people, growing up and getting more freedom means having fun. ▶

When does puberty start?

Puberty can start at any time between the ages of about nine and seventeen. It can take up to five years for your body to change and grow into your adult shape.

The Male and Female Body

Preparing for puberty

It's important to understand how and why your body is changing. It's also important to understand why you might feel happy and positive one day, and miserable and frustrated the next. If you know what to expect, you will find it easier to deal with the changes.

Everyone has a part of their body that they don't really like. Remember that when other people look at you, they see the whole person, not just one feature. ▼

Body shape

A girl's body becomes more rounded during puberty. Breasts grow on her chest and her hips become wider so there is room for a baby to grow during pregnancy. Boys develop broader shoulders. As adults, men tend to be taller than women, with bigger hands and feet.

▲ Each person goes through puberty when their own body is ready. It's important not to tease people who are developing more quickly or slowly than you and your friends.

Male sexual organs

When they are young children, boys and girls look very similar. The main difference you can see is that a boy has a penis and a scrotum, which contains two testicles. These are the boy's external sexual organs. A girl's sexual organs are inside her body (see page 8).

A boy's penis is connected to the bladder and to the testicles. Before puberty, the penis is only used for passing urine. A tube called the urethra runs through the penis from the bladder and carries the urine out of the body.

When a boy reaches puberty, the testicles begin to produce sex cells called sperm. During sex, sperm pass through the penis in a fluid called semen. The semen contains nutrients that the sperm need to stay healthy.

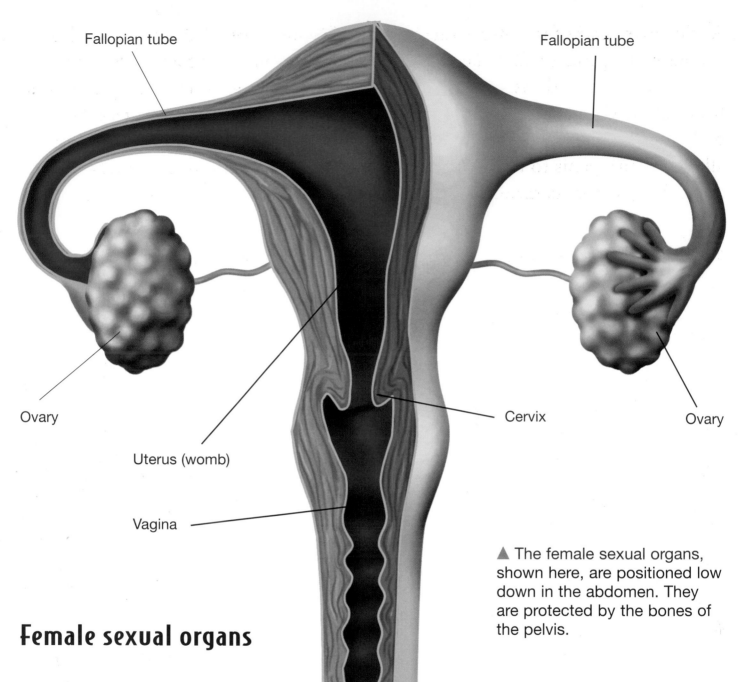

Fallopian tube

Fallopian tube

Ovary

Uterus (womb)

Vagina

Cervix

Ovary

▲ The female sexual organs, shown here, are positioned low down in the abdomen. They are protected by the bones of the pelvis.

Female sexual organs

A girl's sex cells are called ova or eggs. Unlike boys, girls do not produce sex cells throughout their life. All the eggs a girl will ever produce are stored inside her two ovaries when she is born.

Each ovary is linked to the uterus or womb by a Fallopian tube.

Approximately every 28 days, an egg is released from the ovary and travels down the Fallopian tube to the uterus. If it is fertilized by a sperm cell it attaches itself to the side of the uterus and begins to develop into an embryo. The uterus can stretch to around 30 times its normal size as the embryo grows.

At the lower end of the uterus there is a narrow opening called the cervix. A tube called the vagina leads from the cervix to the outside of the body. The vagina can stretch to allow a man's penis to enter it, or so that a baby can pass through it.

The area around the vagina and the urethra (the tube that leads to the bladder) is called the vulva. The labia are folds of skin that protect the entrance to the vagina. In front of the vagina is a tiny organ called the clitoris, which is very sensitive.

This picture has been artificially coloured. It shows an egg being released from the ovary into the fallopian tube. ▼

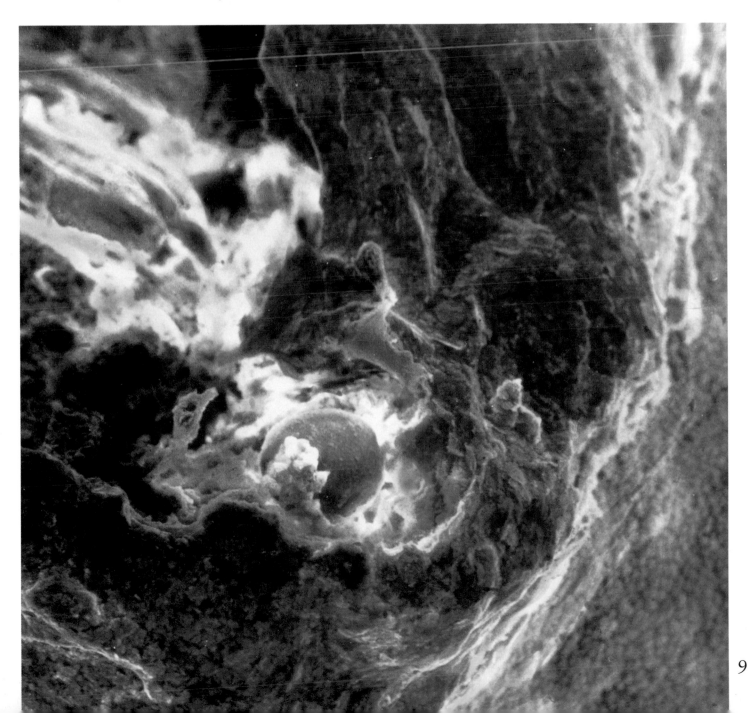

Girls at Puberty

For girls, puberty begins when they start to have periods. However, their body has begun to change even before their periods start.

At around the age of eleven, a girl's ovaries start to produce a hormone called oestrogen. This makes her nipples and breasts grow. It also makes hair grow under her arms and on her lower abdomen.

When she is about thirteen years old, the level of oestrogen in a girl's body begins to rise and fall in a cycle that takes roughly 28 days. This causes the changes inside the sexual organs that make periods happen.

Once they get used to the changes in their body, many girls feel more confident and enjoy looking good. ▶

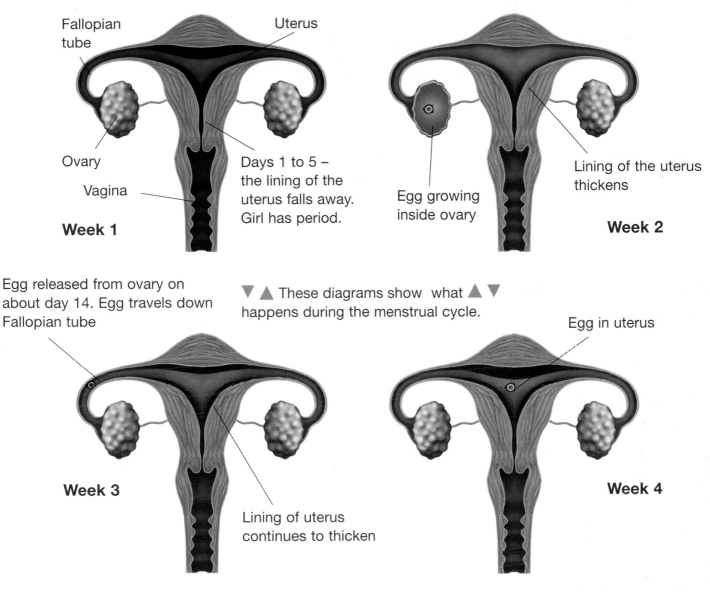

Fallopian tube

Uterus

Ovary

Vagina

Days 1 to 5 – the lining of the uterus falls away. Girl has period.

Week 1

Egg growing inside ovary

Lining of the uterus thickens

Week 2

Egg released from ovary on about day 14. Egg travels down Fallopian tube

▼▲ These diagrams show what ▲▼ happens during the menstrual cycle.

Egg in uterus

Week 3

Lining of uterus continues to thicken

Week 4

The menstrual cycle

The pattern of rising and falling oestrogen levels is called the menstrual cycle. On the first day of the cycle, hormones are released from glands in the brain. One of these hormones makes several eggs in the ovaries start to develop. Another makes the ovaries produce more oestrogen.

What are hormones?

Hormones are chemicals that control processes in the body. They are carried around the body in the blood. Oestrogen is the main hormone that triggers puberty in girls; in boys, the main hormone is testosterone.

11

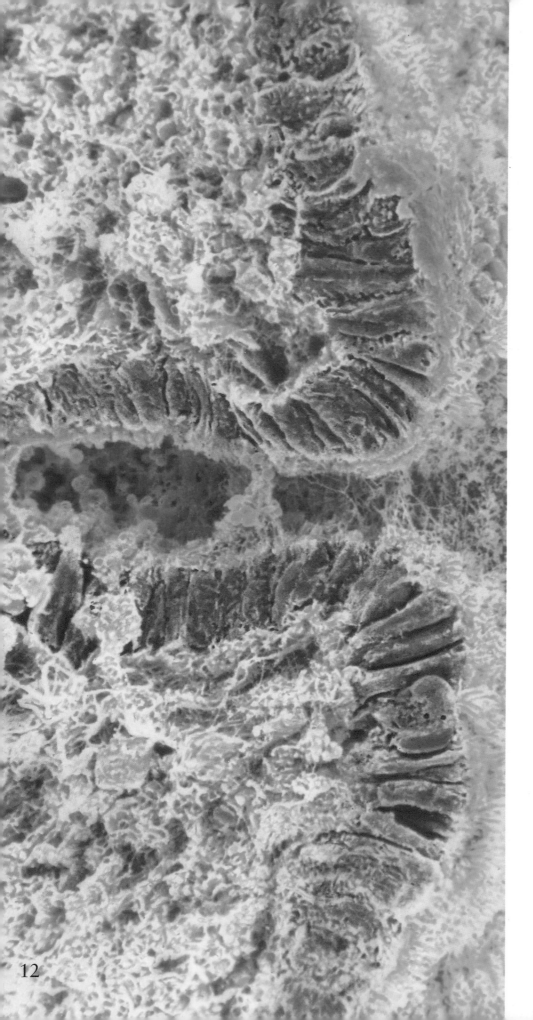

The lining of the uterus starts to thicken on about day 5 of the menstrual cycle. On about day 14, hormone levels reach their peak and trigger the release of an egg from one of the ovaries. This is called ovulation.

The egg travels down the Fallopian tube into the uterus. If it is fertilized by a sperm, it attaches itself to the side of the uterus and begins to develop.

If the egg is not fertilized, the level of hormones drops on around day 28 of the cycle. This causes the lining of the uterus to flow out of the vagina as blood. This is called a period and it usually lasts about five days. The day when the bleeding starts is day 1 of the next cycle.

◄ This artificially coloured picture shows a section of the uterus. The picture was taken on day 22 of the cycle, when the lining of the uterus has thickened.

Some girls feel tired and run down during their period but others are hardly affected at all. Everyone is different. ▶

The risk of pregnancy

An egg can only be fertilized by a sperm in the few days after it leaves the ovary. For this reason, some people think it is safe to have sex without using contraception, as long as they avoid the time near ovulation.

DID YOU KNOW?

Few women have a menstrual cycle that lasts exactly 28 days. When a girl's periods first start, it is common for them to be irregular.

But it is very difficult to be certain when ovulation will take place. If you want to have sex without the risk of pregnancy, you must use reliable contraception (see pages 40–41).

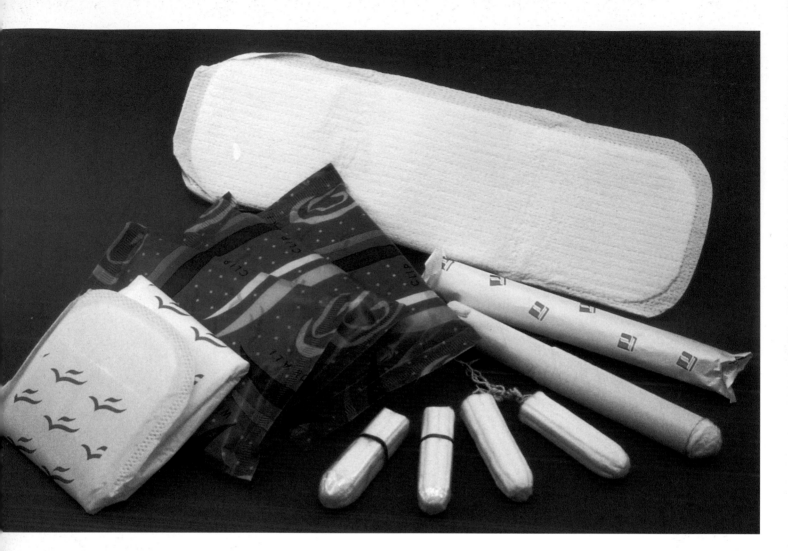

▲ Many different brands of towels and tampons are available. It is worth trying several types to find out which is best for you.

Towels and tampons

Sanitary towels (also called pads) and tampons soak up blood as it flows out of the vagina. Towels can be stuck on to your underwear. Tampons are inserted into your vagina. Different absorbencies are available for days when the flow is heavier or lighter.

It is important to change towels and tampons regularly. It is not a good idea to use a higher absorbency than you need so that you won't need to change as often. Toxic shock syndrome is a rare but serious illness that can develop if tampons are not changed often enough. It is important to follow the instructions on the packet and change a tampon every four to eight hours.

People sweat more during exercise. So washing afterwards is important. ▶

14

Personal hygiene

After puberty, both girls and boys produce sweat that tends to smell more unpleasant than it did when they were younger. The new hormones that your body is producing 'switch on' a set of sweat glands under your arms, around the nipples and between your legs. When bacteria develops and feeds on the sweat produced here, it produces a strong smell. Once you reach puberty, you need to wash more often and perhaps use a deodorant.

Boys at Puberty

Puberty in boys takes place gradually, just as it does in girls. Hormones produced in the brain trigger changes in the testicles. Sperm begin to develop and a hormone called testosterone is produced.

▲ Boys can find some of the changes that take place during puberty embarrassing and difficult to deal with.

Testosterone causes the penis and testicles to grow. It also makes a boy have bigger erections. An erection happens when blood vessels in the penis fill with blood, making the penis bigger and stiffer. Boys can have erections long before puberty, but after puberty they happen more often.

At first, the penis is extra-sensitive to the messages from all the new hormones in the body. Erections can happen unexpectedly, sometimes at times a boy finds embarrassing. Luckily this stage does not last long because the body gradually adjusts to the higher amounts of hormone.

Wet dreams

It is common for men to get erections while they are asleep. Sometimes they ejaculate too, leaving a wet patch on clothes or bedding. This is called a wet dream and it is perfectly normal.

Semen, which contains sperm cells, may be released from the tip of the penis during an erection. This is called ejaculation. If you ejaculate during sex, the sperm travel through the woman's vagina and into the uterus. Your partner could become pregnant. It is essential to use reliable contraception as soon as you start having sex (see pages 40–41).

This picture has been magnified many times. It shows sperm clustering around an egg. Each sperm has a head and a tail. ▼

Body Hair

Testosterone makes hair grow under a boy's arms and around the penis. Later, hair also grows on the face and sometimes on the chest and stomach.

Shaving

The hair that grows on the face appears on the upper lip and chin first. It does not start to grow on the sides of the face until later in adolescence. Some boys start shaving as soon as the hairs are noticeable but others wait until the hair becomes thicker.

Other body changes

Testosterone produces other changes in a boy's body. His muscles grow and his chest becomes broader. The voice box, or larynx, in his throat gets bigger. This makes his voice deeper. As his voice is breaking it sometimes goes squeaky or gruff. Many boys find this embarrassing, especially if other people tease them, but the problem does not last for long.

▲ Many boys worry that they are developing more slowly than their friends but there is nothing you can do to make your body change faster.

Shaving products

Boys often find that their skin gets sore when they start shaving. You might need to experiment with different razors, gels or foams to find the shaving method that is best for you.

If you shave in the direction the hair grows, you are less likely to irritate your skin. ▼

Growth

Boys and girls grow steadily during childhood. On average, they grow about 5cm per year. During adolescence, their growth patterns change.

Growth patterns

When the level of oestrogen in a girl's body begins to rise at the start of puberty, she grows more quickly. Girls grow an average of 9cm per year for between two and four years.

Growth in boys speeds up later than it does in girls. However, boys carry on growing for a year or two longer than girls. By the time they are adults, boys are usually taller.

During adolescence boys and girls grow much faster than their younger brothers and sisters. ▶

20

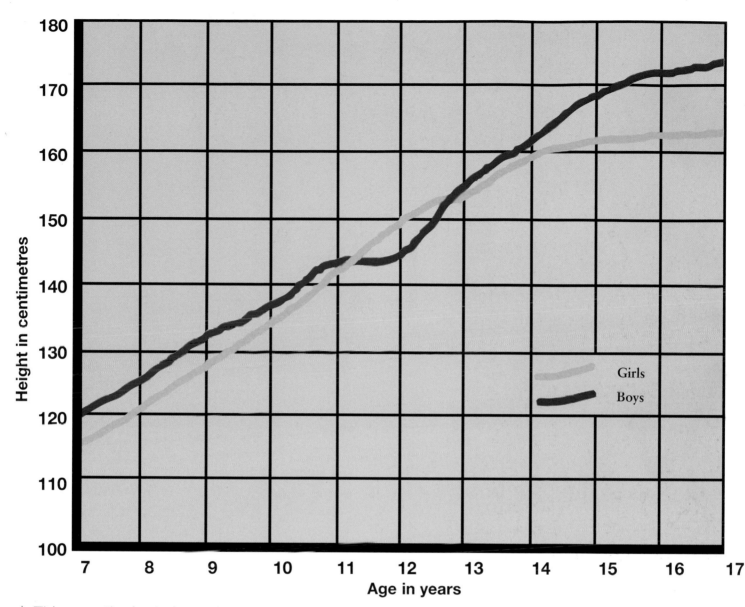

Height in centimetres

Age in years

Girls

Boys

▲ This growth chart shows that girls tend to be taller than boys at around the age of twelve. Boys are taller than girls by their late teens.

Adolescence ends when people stop growing. They have now reached their full adult height. Often, young people grow to roughly the same height as their parents.

What is growth hormone?

Growth hormone is produced in the pituitary gland in the brain. It makes the bones all over the body grow longer. At the end of adolescence, the special growth cells in the bones stop responding to the growth hormone. This is why people stop growing.

Changes inside the body

Growth hormone works on other parts of the body, as well as the bones. It boosts the growth of the muscles and organs such as the heart and lungs. It also changes the way the body releases energy from food. All these changes are designed to make sure that people have enough strength and energy as they grow into adults.

▲ Eating healthy foods will help to keep your body in good shape, even after you have stopped growing.

Healthy diets

People need a diet that includes protein, fat, carbohydrates, vitamins and minerals. If they do not get enough of these nutrients, or too much of some and not enough of others, their body does not grow as well as it should.

This boy is given injections of growth hormone because his body does not produce enough. Doctors check his growth regularly to make sure the treatment is working. ▶

Growth problems

Children are measured regularly to make sure they are growing normally. Sometimes children do not grow as well as they should because they are not eating the right balance of foods, or because their body is not absorbing nutrients properly.

Some children do not produce enough growth hormone to make their bones grow. They can be given injections of growth hormone. It is important to start this treatment as early as possible because even with hormone injections the bones will stop growing at the end of adolescence.

Skin Problems

Adolescence is the time when many young people start to worry about their appearance. It seems really unfair that it is also the time when they start to get skin problems called acne. Some people get away with just a few spots but others suffer from severe acne that affects their neck, back and chest as well as their face.

This diagram shows how the skin is made up below the surface. ▼

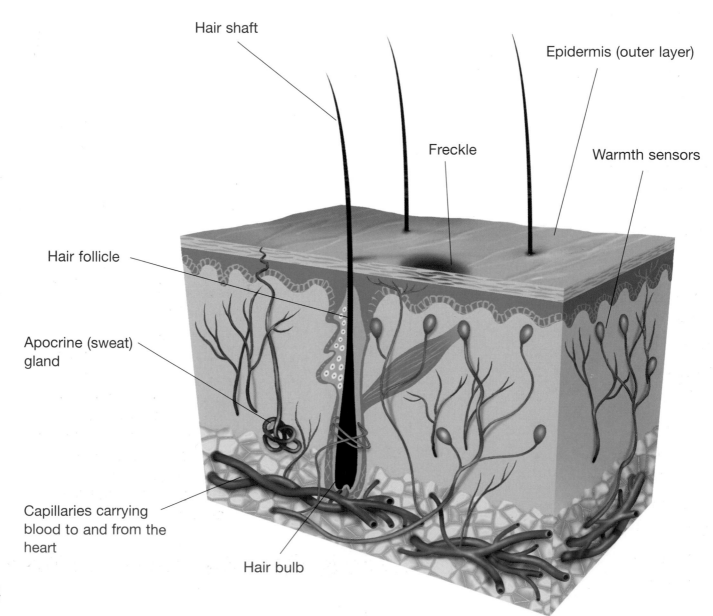

Hair shaft

Epidermis (outer layer)

Freckle

Warmth sensors

Hair follicle

Apocrine (sweat) gland

Capillaries carrying blood to and from the heart

Hair bulb

What causes acne?

At puberty boys start to produce testosterone. Girls produce a little, too. Testosterone makes glands in the skin produce a greasy substance called sebum. It oozes on to the surface of the skin through tiny tubes.

When the glands are first activated, they produce too much sebum. The tiny tubes, called follicles, become blocked and the sebum cannot escape. It forms a solid plug, which develops into a blackhead, whitehead or spot.

It is important to treat acne to prevent scarring. ▶

What makes a spot?

A spot forms when bacteria on the surface of the skin break down the greasy plugs in the follicles (see box above). Chemicals are released that make the skin red. A swelling develops, sometimes filled with yellowish pus. Eventually it bursts or shrinks and the spot heals.

How can you treat acne?

Many of the acne treatments you can buy from the pharmacy contain benzoyl peroxide. This chemical works by cutting down the amount of sebum the glands produce. It also reduces the amount of bacteria on the skin. It won't cure your acne overnight, though – you need to carry on using it for six to eight weeks. If your skin becomes very sore, stop using it and ask your pharmacist or doctor for advice.

Helping yourself

If you have acne, it doesn't mean you have an unhealthy diet or don't wash properly. It just means your skin is extra-sensitive to testosterone. Using an anti-bacterial wash instead of ordinary soap can help, but it is not a good idea to wash many times a day. This will just make your skin dry and sore.

Eating fatty foods, smoking and drinking alcohol will not give you acne but will not help your skin to stay healthy either. Drinking plenty of water and eating fresh fruit and vegetables will help your skin to look better. If acne is making you feel miserable, you can buy creams that help to cover the spots.

Help from the doctor

If treatments such as benzoyl peroxide don't clear your spots, get advice from your doctor. Antibiotic cream or tablets destroy the bacteria that cause the pus-filled spots. This treatment can take several months to work. Girls can use a particular type of contraceptive pill that reduces the amount of sebum produced in the skin. This treatment takes at least a year.

Fruit contains vitamins and minerals that help your skin to stay healthy. ▶

Other treatments

If you have severe acne, your doctor might arrange for you to see a skin specialist at a hospital. Some acne treatments can make the skin very dry or affect other parts of the body, so it is important to get expert advice.

◀ A pharmacist can tell you which acne treatments work best.

Emotions

It is not just your body that changes during adolescence. The hormones that are making you look different are also changing the way you think and feel. Your moods can swing from one extreme to another very quickly. You might feel happy, sad, angry and excited – all before morning break!

▲ Finding a boyfriend or girlfriend can be one of the exciting new experiences of adolescence.

Making new friends

Before adolescence, many girls think boys are stupid and a lot of boys think the same about girls. During adolescence, these attitudes usually change! Teenage girls and boys start to spend more time together. They might form a large group of friends to begin with, perhaps because they like the same music. Sometimes, two people like each other very much and become a couple.

It's important not to lose touch with your old friends once you become part of a couple. ▶

Feeling left out

If your friend has a boyfriend or girlfriend, they will probably want to spend a lot of time together. You might feel hurt and left out. Talk to your friend about how you feel but try to understand their feelings too. Soon it might be your turn to get excited about a new boyfriend or girlfriend.

Share your feelings

Dealing with the many emotions you are feeling is not easy. It can be like riding a rollercoaster – up one minute, down the next. To make things even more complicated, your friends are going through the same experiences. Sharing your feelings can help because then you know you are not the only one having problems.

Negotiating with parents

Your parents will probably worry less about you if you show them that you have thought your plans through. If you want to stay out later at night, for example, your parents might be willing to agree, as long as you tell them where you are going and how you are planning to get home. Carry a mobile phone so that you can contact your parents if your plans change.

Trouble at home

Many young people feel that they are always in trouble during adolescence. Perhaps parents don't like their clothes or friends. There might be arguments about staying out too late, not spending enough time on schoolwork – almost anything really! As people change from children into adults, they begin to want the independence that adults enjoy. Adolescents want to make their own decisions about the things they do.

Parents, on the other hand, often worry that their children don't yet have the skills or experience to make sensible – or safe – decisions. It can be hard for them to accept that their children are growing up.

◀ Teenagers often feel resentful when parents tell them what to do.

Arguments at home can make life miserable but you can be sure that you are not the only teenager whose parents get annoyed. ▼

Feeling tearful all the time is not a normal part of adolescence – it is a symptom of depression.

Depression

It's common to feel sad or frustrated some of the time during adolescence. However, young people who feel low most of the time may be suffering from depression. Other symptoms include finding it hard to sleep or concentrate, and getting a lot of minor aches and pains. Don't ignore these feelings. Ask your doctor for help.

Eating disorders

Some adolescents develop problems with food. People who starve themselves but still think that they look fat have a disorder called anorexia nervosa. People with bulimia nervosa eat a lot of food all in one go and immediately make themselves sick so they won't put on weight. Compulsive eaters eat a lot of food and then diet to try to lose weight.

What causes eating disorders?

People sometimes develop eating disorders because they are very worried about the way they look. Some people control the food they eat as a way of dealing with some deep unhappiness in their life. Specially trained therapists can try to find out what emotional problems are causing the eating disorder and help people to deal with them. People with severe anorexia have to be treated in hospital.

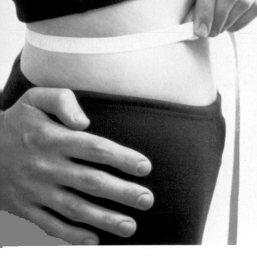

▲ Girls sometimes become desperate to look as slim as the models they see in magazines.

DID YOU KNOW?

Boys as well as girls suffer from eating disorders. Experts estimate that around 25 per cent of teenagers with eating disorders are boys.

Anorexia can damage organs such as the heart and kidneys. It makes the bones weak, so they break easily. Having children becomes more difficult, or impossible. People with severe anorexia can die.

Getting help

Your family and friends may not know enough about your problem to help you tackle it. Contact one of the organizations listed on page 47 for more advice.

Talking to a friend or family member can be the first step in getting help and support.

Drink and drugs

Trying out new experiences is an important part of adolescence. It only becomes a problem if you are experimenting with things that are bad for you, or illegal.

Drinking alcohol or taking drugs might make you feel good at first, especially if a lot of your friends are doing the same thing. However, you need to be aware of the dangers. For example, it is rare for people to die as a result of taking ecstasy but each year the number of deaths related to ecstasy is increasing. Every year, about 1,000 children aged under fifteen are admitted to hospital needing emergency treatment for acute alcohol poisoning.

▲ You might think smoking looks cool but it also makes your breath, hair and clothes smell terrible.

Smoking kills

One cigarette won't give you lung cancer, but once you start smoking it becomes very hard to stop. Your lungs will soon become swollen and sore. Taking exercise will be more of a struggle. About half the people who smoke regularly die of diseases caused by cigarettes.

Sex

Magazines, TV programmes and films can make it seem as though all teenagers start having sex as soon as they reach puberty. But even if people have a boyfriend or girlfriend, it doesn't necessarily mean that they are ready for a sexual relationship.

Getting the message

Nerves carry messages from the skin to the brain. There are a lot of nerve endings in some parts of the body, such as the face, breasts and genitals. When you touch or stroke these areas, your brain receives the message that it feels good. After puberty, the sex hormones in the blood make these areas extra sensitive.

◄ You should never feel pressured into having sex if you don't feel ready for it.

Some people boast about having sex with a person they have only just met, but sex is usually better as part of a long-term, loving relationship. Many people need to feel relaxed with their partner before they become physically close. It's much easier to relax if you are with someone you know well and trust.

Touching and stroking each other can make you feel good, but only if you both feel comfortable about what you are doing. If one of you feels nervous or scared, you won't get much pleasure from it.

Getting to know each other is the first step in a relationship. ▼

Pleasing yourself

Even before having sex with a partner, many young people like to explore their own body to find out what feels good. Most people get pleasure from touching and stroking their penis or clitoris, providing they feel relaxed about it. This is called masturbation. It is perfectly normal, although it's not a good idea to do it in front of other people – they may feel embarrassed or even threatened.

▲ There is no need to feel guilty about masturbation. Most people do it.

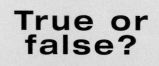

Masturbation is harmful.

False. Masturbation does not damage your health in any way. However, if you do it very often or rub too hard you will make yourself sore.

Waiting for marriage

Some people believe it is important to wait until you are married before you have sex. This may be because of their religious beliefs, or because they think it is the best way to prevent unwanted pregnancies and sexually transmitted diseases.

The closer you feel, the more enjoyable sex will be. ▼

Getting closer

For some couples, kissing, cuddling and touching are enough. They choose not to take their relationship any further. Others spend weeks or months getting to know each other's bodies before they actually have sex. There are no rules to say how long you should spend at one stage before moving on to the next.

Like most activities, sex gets better with practice. It takes time to find out what you like and what your partner enjoys. If your partner doesn't like a particular kind of touching or way of having sex, it is wrong to bully or force them into it.

Choosing contraception

Many couples find it difficult to discuss contraception. It is vital that you tackle this issue though. If you use contraception properly, you can avoid an unwanted pregnancy. Some contraceptives will also protect you from the diseases that can be passed from one person to another during sex, including HIV/AIDS.

It's difficult to relax and have fun if you are worrying about pregnancy. So it's always best to use contraception. ▼

Condoms

A condom fits over the penis and prevents sperm from entering the vagina. You can buy condoms from pharmacies, shops and vending machines in public toilets.

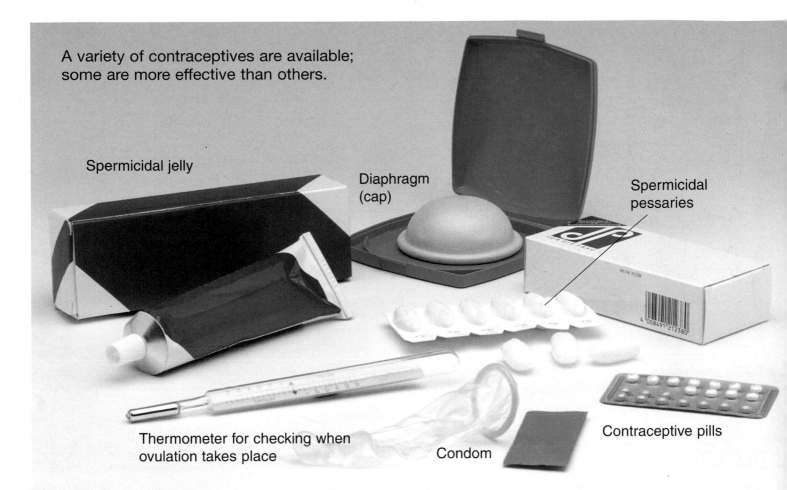

A variety of contraceptives are available; some are more effective than others.

Spermicidal jelly

Diaphragm (cap)

Spermicidal pessaries

Thermometer for checking when ovulation takes place

Condom

Contraceptive pills

Unreliable methods

Taking the penis out of the vagina before the man comes, or ejaculates, is not an effective way to prevent pregnancy. This is because a tiny amount of semen, which contains sperm, often trickles out of the penis before ejaculation.

Some people try to avoid pregnancy by not having sex around the time of ovulation. The problem is that it is

The Pill

The Pill releases hormones into the body to prevent the ovaries from releasing an egg or make it difficult for an egg to be fertilized and develop into an embryo. You need a doctor's prescription to get the Pill. You have to take the Pill each day, usually for three weeks out of four. If you forget to take it you may not be protected from pregnancy.

very difficult to be sure when an egg has been released, especially in young women who may not have a regular menstrual cycle.

Unrolling a condom and putting it on properly can be tricky until you get used to it. It's a good idea to practise first! ▶

Sexual health

It's a good idea to use a condom even if you are on the Pill. Since the mid-1990s there has been a huge rise in the numbers of young people infected with sexually transmitted diseases. Condoms can protect you from catching and passing on infections.

Pregnancy

If you become pregnant accidentally, you will face some difficult decisions. You might decide to end the pregnancy by having an abortion. You could have the baby and then give it to another family to bring up as their own. Or your own family might help you to bring up your baby. This might mean giving up school – and nights out with your friends.

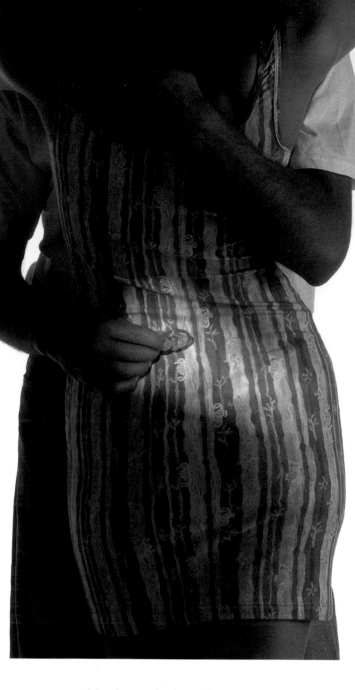

Having a baby when you are young might mean giving up or postponing plans to go to college, or get a particular job. ▶

How to get help

If you think you are pregnant or have a sexually transmitted disease, there are people who can help you. Some useful organizations are listed on page 47.

Under Pressure

People often feel that they are under a lot of pressure during adolescence. Parents and teachers, for instance, usually want you to work hard at school and do as well as you possibly can. You might worry that you will be letting them down if you don't get top grades in all your exams. You might feel resentful because they are planning your future before you really know yourself what you want. Make sure you keep talking to your parents so they understand how you feel.

Many teenagers worry about whether they will pass their exams. ▼

Really good friends don't put pressure on you to do things that make you feel uncomfortable. ▶

Other pressures can come from friends. You might feel you have to dress in a particular way or listen to certain music in order to be accepted by them. They might put pressure on you to take part in risky activities such as smoking, drinking alcohol or taking drugs. Often, it's much harder to say 'no' to your friends than to your parents. True friends will respect any decision you make, though, and won't try to persuade you to do anything you don't want to do.

'It's my life!'

Trying out different activities and making new friends is how you find out what your real interests and opinions are. As you become more confident, it will be easier to resist pressure from others. In the meantime, the organizations listed on page 47 can offer you support.

Glossary

abortion The deliberate ending of a pregnancy.

adolescence The time of rapid physical and emotional development that marks the change from child to adult.

bladder The part of the body where urine is stored before it leaves the body.

contraception The general word for the different methods of preventing pregnancy.

contraceptive A particular method of preventing pregnancy, such as a condom.

counselling Talking through a problem with a specially trained adviser.

depression Feeling very unhappy and worthless over a long period of time.

diaphragm A 'cap' that fits over the cervix to prevent sperm entering the uterus.

ejaculation The spurting of semen from the penis (often described as 'coming').

embryo A baby in the early stages of development in the uterus.

fertilize To make an egg capable of developing into a baby as a result of the egg joining with a sperm cell.

foetus A baby in the later stages of development in the uterus.

genitals The sex organs on the outside of the body – the penis and testicles in a boy and the vulva in a girl.

gland A part of the body that produces hormones and other fluids.

HIV/AIDS A disease passed on through contact with infected body fluids such as blood, saliva or semen; there is no cure.

hormone A chemical produced by the body that controls body processes.

menstrual cycle The pattern of changes that take place in a girl's sex organs approximately every 28 days, as her body prepares for a possible pregnancy .

ovulation The release of an egg from one of the ovaries.

period *(also called menstruation)*, Bleeding from the vagina that occurs roughly every 28 days, when the lining of the uterus breaks down .

puberty The body changes that take place in boys and girls to make them capable of producing a baby.

scrotum The 'bag' of skin behind the penis that contains the testicles.

sebum Oil produced by glands in the skin.

sexually transmitted diseases Diseases passed through body fluids during sexual contact; these include HIV/AIDS, chlamydia, gonorrhea and syphilis.

sperm The male sex cell.

spermicide A chemical that kills sperm; it can be used with a condom in the form of a cream, jelly, or pessary.

testicles The parts of the male sex organs that produce sperm.

testosterone The hormone produced in the testicles that results in changes to a boy's body at puberty; girls also produce a little testosterone.

urine Waste products that pass out of the body as liquid.

Finding Out More

Books to read

Everything You Ever Wanted to Ask about Willies by Tricia Kreitman, Dr Neil Simpson, Dr Rosemary Jones (Piccadilly Press, 2002)

Flirtology by Anita Naik (Hodder Children's Books, 2005)

Get Real: Coping with Your Emotions by Kate Tym (Raintree, 2004)

Have You Started Yet? By Ruth Thomson (Macmillan Children's Books, 1995)

Health Issues: Pregnancy by Kirsten Lamb (Wayland, 2004)

Health Issues: Sexually Transmitted Diseases by Jo Whelan (Wayland, 2002)

The Puberty Book by Wendy Darvill and Kelsey Powell (Newleaf, 2001)

Teenage Health Freak: Sex by Ann McPherson and Aidan Macfarlane (Oxford University Press, 2003)

Useful Organizations

Alcohol Concern
Waterbridge House
32-36 Loman Street,
London SE1 0EE
Tel: 020 7928 7377
Fax: 020 7928 4644

Brook
421 Highgate Studios
53-79 Highgate Road
London NW5 1TL
Tel: 020 7284 6040
Fax: 020 7284 6050
http://www.brook.org.uk
Brook clinics are found around the country. They provide advice on sex and contraception; the website has links to many other useful agencies.

ChildLine
Tel: 0800 1111
www.childline.org.uk
A free, confidential helpline for children in distress, whether as a result of bullying, abuse or any other reason.

Drinkline
0800 917 82 82
A free helpline providing advice on problems related to alcohol

Young Minds
Young Minds Parents' Information Service:
0800 018 2138
(Mon, Fri 10am-1pm; Tues-Thurs 1-4pm)
This charity works to improve the mental health of children and young people.

Index